THE PIAN

Felix Mendelssohn

Eleven favourite pieces

The Piano Music of
Felix Mendelssohn

THE PIANO MUSIC OF
Felix Mendelssohn
Eleven favourite pieces

Kevin Mayhew

We hope you enjoy *The Piano Music of Felix Mendelssohn*.
Further copies of this and the other books in the series
are available from your local music shop.

In case of difficulty, please contact the publisher direct:

The Sales Department
KEVIN MAYHEW LTD
Rattlesden
Bury St Edmunds
Suffolk IP30 0SZ

Phone 01449 737978
Fax 01449 737834

Please ask for our complete catalogue of outstanding Instrumental Music.

Front Cover: *A Quartette* by Frederick Daniel Hardy (1825-1911).
Courtesy of Fine Art Photographic Library Ltd, London.
Reproduced by kind permission.

Cover designed by Graham Johnstone and Veronica Ward.

First published in Great Britain in 1992 and 1993 by Kevin Mayhew Ltd

This compilation © Copyright 1996 Kevin Mayhew Ltd

ISBN 0 86209 734 7
Catalogue No: 3611186

Printed and bound in Great Britain
by Caligraving Limited Thetford Norfolk

Contents

BARCAROLLE

Felix Mendelssohn (1809-1847)

9

CAVATINA

Felix Mendelssohn (1809-1847)

SCHERZO

Felix Mendelssohn (1809-1847)

CANZONA

Felix Mendelssohn (1809-1847)

ADAGIO

Felix Mendelssohn (1809-1847)

ANDANTE CON MOTO

Felix Mendelssohn (1809-1847)

MEDITATION

Felix Mendelssohn (1809-1847)

ALLEGRETTO

Felix Mendelssohn (1809-1847)

ANDANTE SOSTENUTO

Felix Mendelssohn (1809-1847)

ROMANCE

Felix Mendelssohn (1809-1847)

PASTORALE

Felix Mendelssohn (1809-1847)